On Jesus at
Twelve Years Old

THE COLUMBA SERIES

Saint Aelred of Rievaulx

On Jesus at
Twelve Years Old

Translated from the Latin by
GEOFFREY WEBB AND ADRIAN WALKER

London
The Saint Austin Press
MMI

Nihil Obstat: HUBERTUS RICHARDS, S.T.L., L.S.S.
Imprimatur: E. MORROGH BERNARD, *Vic. Gen.*
Westmonasterii, die 19a Julii, 1955

The Saint Austin Press
296 Brockley Road
London
SE4 2RA
Tel +44 (0)20 8692 6009
Fax +44 (0)20 8469 3609
Email: books@saintaustin.org
Website: www.saintaustin.org

ISBN 1901157 51 2

First published by Mowbrays in 1956

Design and typography of this edition © The Saint Austin Press, 2001.

Printed by Newton Design & Print Ltd, London, UK.   www.newtondp.co.uk

CONTENTS

INTRODUCTION

AELRED OF RIEVAULX was by birth completely English.
His ancestry connected him with the church in Northumbria for many generations past, and with distinguished
families in the area of Hexham and Durham. He was born
in 1110, the son of Eilaf, priest of Hexham, a learned,
respectable and conscientious man. It is easy to see why the
movement for a celibate clergy progressed so slowly at that
time, if there were many such men as Eilaf.

Though he was not trained in the schools of France, it is
clear that Aelred had been taught well, probably at Hexham.
In late boyhood he became one of the court circle of King
David of Scotland, where he was the companion of David's
two boys. When he was older, Aelred realized that the king
might have ruined his life, had he not been a truly Christian
man. But the Scottish court had a tradition of sanctity,
starting with Saint Margaret, as well as a long record of
courage, so that Aelred's character must have been strengthened greatly in such an atmosphere.

The crises which tormented Saint Augustine's intellect
did not affect him, but he was held by strong ties of ambition
and affection, just as the great bishop of Hippo had been.
It was his heart that held him back from his heart's resting
place, and he tells us that the bonds of friendship shackled
him, especially one which was the greatest delight in his
life at that time. For a long period he fought with himself,
and death often seemed the only way to avoid the yoke
which pressed so hard on him.

About 1134 King David sent Aelred on a mission to
Archbishop Thurstan of York. The young courtier and his
companions stayed the night with Walter Espec, who two

years before had founded a monastery of Cistercians in the
valley of the Rie (hence the name Rievaulx). Walter spoke
of their life of austerity and of their sublime ideals, and
Aelred's heart burned with admiration and enthusiasm. It
was next day that the company from Scotland visited the
new monastery, and after another night with Walter they
set out again on their return journey northwards. One of
Aelred's companions wished to visit the monks again, and
so they went down into the valley together. No longer
could Aelred resist, and after spending three days in the
guest house, as is the custom with the white monks, he was
received into the noviciate. He was just twenty-four years
old.

Cistercian life to this young courtier was bleak. He had
to live with short hours of sleep, long hours of prayer and
work, and on a scanty diet. His eyes were restless and his
heart was ready to receive every impression; to overcome
his difficulties, he immediately threw himself into the study
of sacred scripture. At last he had found a place of perfect
peace of mind and heart. But his character underwent no
violent change, for throughout his life he kept his warm
readiness to give and to receive love. And his love embraced
all who would accept it, although it was as unique for each
as that of a mother for every one of her children.

The years he had spent in the Scottish court must have
given his bearing distinction, and as a young man he was
unusually handsome. William, the first abbot of Rievaulx
and a friend of Saint Bernard, soon discovered that his new
recruit was a man of ability. His past history and the
qualities of his mind, in addition to his increasing sanctity,
prompted the abbot to use him often on journeys for the
abbey. In 1142, Aelred was appointed novice master, an
office which he held for only one year. The work he wrote
while instructing those in his care on the religious life, the

Mirror of Charity, is a lasting record of his tenure of that responsible position. And when his biographer wrote, some of his novices were still living 'to testify, as much by the sweetness of their character as by the living voice, to his praiseworthy industry. Their manner of life is such that they seem to bear blossoms more dazzling white than the white flowers about them, and they reveal a yet greater loveliness of incomparable grace.' Only a year later he was appointed first abbot of the colony of monks who set out to make a new foundation at Revesby in Lincolnshire. He was then thirty-three.

In 1145 Abbot William died, and his place was taken at Rievaulx by Maurice, 'a man of great sanctity and outstanding judgment,' whose distinguished life and learning caused him to be compared with Bede the Venerable. But he resigned after two years, and Aelred was chosen to succeed him.

A Cistercian abbot is not the lord, but rather the father of his community, and the spiritual director of all his monks. And Aelred now became, to more than three hundred monks and lay brothers, what he had been five years before to a few novices. Under his rule, the life at Rievaulx was observant, austere and truly spiritual, for there his gifts of mind and soul found their full scope. Rievaulx in his time was the source of that strong Cistercian influence which came into play in English life. Around York, Aelred's name was famous and powerful, for he was one of the most important and influential people north of the Trent.

But his life was not always peaceful and quiet, even when he was sheltered in his abbey. His community was large already when he was made superior, and it grew quickly because he was never willing to turn applicants away. The huge estates were farmed by many lay brothers and servants, so that on feast days the church was packed with religious as a hive is crowded with bees, his biographer says. And since he was convinced that his rule should be mild, it must have been due principally to his influence that life at Rievaulx was so happy and calm. His energies would have been sapped by business and administration, his body tired by the long journeys on visitation to his daughter-houses, and by the daily round and routine which his office imposed on him. And as he grew older, this monk, who was so saintly and yet so completely human, loved to recall his youth and the friends which, he said, were the world's most precious gift to him.

It was the personal direction of Aelred that built up the large family of the house. The community may have numbered three hundred when he was appointed novice master in 1142, but in 1165, just over a year before he died, the number had risen to about six hundred and fifty. These men came not only in answer to the call of Cistercian life, but also at Aelred's express invitation and desire. Clearly, for him, the life was not merely for certain chosen souls, but a home for every kind of man. He said that Rievaulx must be a haven of charity for every type of character, and a world in miniature. He thought of monastic profession as a soul's dedication to the love of God, whereby the soul, searching for God, could achieve a real and conscious union with its Maker. And so it was that Rievaulx became the abode of perfect love of God and neighbour.

We must remember that most of those who answered Aelred's invitation were lay brothers, untaught, and of peasant stock, while others were learned young men who had attended the schools. Some were shackled by the ties of sin. Others were pure and innocent, like Aelred's young friend, Simon. Some had been brought up in comfort, while others were already used to a hard life. Aelred had to watch them all in order to find out how best to train them.

He had to find the right remedy for every sin and bad habit he found among them. Every man who came there found a loving father in Aelred, and helpers and comforters among the brethren. And although so many came to Rievaulx, no one was ever sent away in Aelred's time, for he held that if a house is too proud to bear with its weaker brethren, it cannot be called a house of religion. He claimed that Rievaulx was outstanding, because, above all other houses, it had learned to have compassion on all in their needs.

It is easy to see how dangerous are such convictions as this one, and Aelred did not escape the censure of visiting abbots. None the less, Rievaulx did maintain, for many years after Aelred's death, the fervent observance which had existed during his lifetime.

During all his years as abbot, the beauty of Aelred's friendships shone undimmed. It was these, perhaps, which helped him most to understand life and its meaning, adding to its reality and value. Even amid the concerns and occupations of his office, he still tried to be with those he loved for a few brief minutes whenever time allowed. His friends gave him cheerful company when he was tired and depressed. They urged him on when the way seemed hard. Above all, it was they who encouraged him in his writing.

Aelred's works fall into two divisions, spiritual and historical. His historical treatises are full of the traditions of Bede the Venerable, and are typically the work of a northerner from the same area as that great doctor of the church. He wrote the lives of Saint Ninian and Saint Edward the Confessor, together with a tract on the battle of the Standard, and a genealogy of the kings of England. It was after this last-named work that he wrote the treatise which we here offer in translation. Of his spiritual writings, the two most outstanding are the *Mirror of Charity* and *On Spiritual Friendship*, in which he shows with overwhelming sincerity how his own mind and heart had advanced from the human to the divine. It is this characteristic which makes him quite unique in England or abroad, and without his like even among the contemporary white monks. His touch is sure, his self-expression is completely original, while it is clear from his work that he was quietly certain of himself, though at the same time knowing the weaknesses and qualities of his hearers.

Aelred was not a deep or speculative theologian, for his writings merely reflect the thought of his time. But his spiritual dialogues are much indebted to great exemplars like Cicero's work *On Friendship*, and Saint Augustine's *Confessions*. For Aelred was almost the only man in his time, and for many years to come, to approach his Augustine through the *Confessions*. It was the man that interested him, not the thinker, the preacher, or the theologian. Aelred realized that he shared with Augustine a companionship of deep emotion and feeling, and he saw in him a guide for his own journey from the world to God.

It was about 1143 that he began to open a voluminous correspondence, in which, his biographer tells us, 'he left a living image of himself, for what he there commended in writing, he himself practised in life, and lived much better than he could say.' Men of every grade and position received letters from him—the pope, kings, bishops, and men throughout the kingdom. Unfortunately, all of these epistles have been lost, except for the few which form prefaces to his works.

Even a man in perfect health would have felt the strain which sapped the energy of mind and body in Aelred, for the demands of his many duties and commitments taxed him to the uttermost. But, in addition to this, he was constantly ill. He suffered from a disease which made him unable to move, and even the gentlest touch gave him most acute pain. Added to that were frequent attacks of the stone, which forced him to lie down for long periods. During these spasms of pain, 'his body, looking—as he lay by the fire—like a leaf of parchment. He was so bent that his head seemed altogether lost between his knees.'

For the last ten years of his life he availed himself of a dispensation which the general chapter had granted him. He was allowed to live in the infirmary, but this did not mean that he was to go into retirement, for he was still allowed to travel about his estates and outlying granges when he was able, and to take as full a part as he could in all the duties of the monastery. He might sing mass both in public and private, recite the hours of divine office where he preferred, and go to choir at times different from those prescribed for other abbots. But he felt diffident about this generous provision, and so he ordered a little thatched hut to be built for him alongside the infirmary. This he called his 'mausoleum,' and had it divided into two parts. In one part he had a little oratory where he did his writing and spent hours in prayer. In the other half he welcomed those who came to visit him, 'walking or sitting about his bed, and talking with him as little children prattle with their mother'. He would sit for hours in this little house, crouching by the fire to relieve his pain, and reading the books he loved so much, Saint John's gospel, and the *Confessions* of 'his' Augustine. So absorbed did he become that the hours for office and meals often slipped by without his noticing them. As his illness increased he became more austere, but in no way less human, and he rejected any curatives, 'giving little weight to the counsels of physicians, and considering in all ways the health of the soul.'

His life began to draw to a close on Christmas Eve, 1166, and a few days later he said a formal farewell to his monks. Calling God to witness, he said that, since his entry into

religion, no strong feeling against any man had remained
in his heart beyond the waning of any day. 'God Who
knows all things knows that I love you all as myself, and, as
earnestly as a mother for her sons, I long for you all with
the tenderness of Jesus Christ Himself.' His monks, even as
many as a hundred, crowded around his bed, so much did
they admire and love him. And Aelred, in his turn, thought
that this was the greatest and best of all God's blessings,
'that he should be chosen by God and men to be so well
beloved.'

He was anointed with the holy oils and fortified by holy
viaticum at the hands of Roger, abbot of Byland. And on
the day before he died, Roger was by his side again with
Richard, the abbot of Fountains, most of the monks, and
a few lay brothers. The Passion was read aloud, and
because he was unable to speak he followed the words in
his heart. One of his monks, Walter Daniel, who afterwards
wrote the biography of this great saint, took Aelred's head
in his hands and said, 'Father, gaze on the cross, and let your
eye be where your heart is.' And Aelred turned to look at
the crucifix, saying, 'Thou art my God and my Lord,
Thou art my refuge and my salvation. Thou art my glory
and my hope for evermore. Into Thy hands I commend my
spirit.' Those were his last words.

And so he died on January 12th, 1167, with his monks
about him as he lay, according to the ancient monastic
custom, on sackcloth and ashes. Walter Daniel helped to
prepare the body for burial, and he anointed the thumb,
index and middle finger of Aelred's hand with balsam,
because it was with these that so many beautiful things
about God had been written. 'Never before in life,' we
read, 'was that fair and seemly man habited in flesh so
bright as when he lay in death.'

When all was over, there were inevitably some who

decried Aelred's life and work, accusing him of ambition and comfortable living, and saying that he was a bootlicker and a hypocrite. To combat such suggestions, Walter Daniel wrote a life of Aelred which springs from his deep and loving devotion to the great abbot who had been his father for so many years. 'My hearers may laugh, they may mock at my words, they may throw my writing in the fire, they may do as they please. But I hold fast to this—that Aelred's charity, based on purity of heart, a good conscience and a sincere faith, exceeded every novelty of miracle.'

. . . . .

The devotional treatise *On Jesus at twelve years old* was written by Aelred sometime between 1153 and 1157 for Ivo, a monk of Wardon, who may have been sent to this house from Rievaulx about 1135. We see Ivo in the dialogue on friendship as a gentle person, devoted to study, and passionately fond of Aelred. They would seem to have shared the same devotion to our Lord in His boyhood, and it is known that Aelred never spoke of the finding in the temple without particular joy.

The subject of the gospel which Aelred expounds in this work is rich enough to provide him with several trains of thought—or rather with a train of thought which can be developed under several aspects and at different levels. Firstly, there is the literal exposition of the text, in which he fills in imaginatively the details which Saint Luke does not record. Thus we have the questions in the first chapter . . . Where did He lodge? Whose company did He enjoy? And in the fourth chapter we find a delightful reconstruction of the journey to the holy city.

Secondly, Aelred sees in the search of Mary and Joseph for their child an allegory of the synagogue as it seeks for the Holy One of Israel, Who has taken up His abode in the church of the Gentiles. This is described in chapters

eight to ten. After the allegorical interpretation of the text
Aelred sets out the spiritual meaning as applied to Christ's
work of Redemption. In chapter three we see how He
spent the three days mystically with His Father, the angels,
and the patriarchs, submitting Himself to the Father's will,
and rejoicing all the hosts of heaven with His promise to
rebuild the ruin left by the fallen angels. The patriarchs and
prophets are consoled by the assurance that He will soon
take them into heaven with Him, after overcoming the
powers of darkness.

This spiritual interpretation concerns all mankind, but
now we come to the most important sense in which Ivo is
to understand the gospel story. The life of Christ, from
Bethlehem to Nazareth, and from Nazareth to Jerusalem,
is treated as a figure of the soul's conversion and journey to
God. Before Bethlehem, we are all 'prodigal sons' who
have wasted our substance in a far country—a country, that
is, far removed from God. We leave the country of hunger
and thirst, and make our way to Bethlehem, the 'house of
bread.' This is described in chapters two and three. After
the persecution of Herod we come, as Christ did, to Nazareth, the 'city of flowers.' Aelred compares these flowers to
the beginnings of virtue, as opposed to the fruits which the
soul will produce later in Jerusalem.

It is when we come to Jerusalem that 'we receive the
grace to contemplate the secrets of heaven.' And it is here
that the gifts of the Holy Spirit are bestowed on us, and the
desire for Jesus becomes stronger, as Aelred tells us in
chapter twelve; while in the next chapter he compares the
contemplation of God in His attributes of power, wisdom,
and goodness, to a threefold light. This is brought into
the pattern of the three days, followed in the previous
interpretations.

In the final chapter, which tells of the finding in the

temple, all four strands of interpretation find their resolution. Mary and Joseph find the Son of God, as does all humanity, and each soul in its longing. The parents of Jesus provide an image of the mysterious parentage of the Holy Spirit and Charity, acting through the religious superior in respect of his spiritual children. And ultimately the synagogue, too, the 'house of Jacob, will echò with shouts of gladness and rejoicing.'

For permission to quote from Walter Daniel's *Life of Aelred*, edited by F. M. Powicke (1950) in the series 'Mediaeval Classics,' we have to thank Messrs. Thomas Nelson & Sons, who have also kindly allowed us to use quotations from the Revised Standard Version of the Holy Bible. We are also indebted to His Eminence the Cardinal Archbishop of Westminster and to Messrs. Burns, Oates & Washbourne for permission to quote from Monsignor Knox's translation of the scriptures.

G. W.

Feast of Saint Mary of Scotland   A. W.

Now the parents of Jesus went to Jerusalem every year at the feast of the Passover. And when He was twelve years old, they went up according to custom; and when the feast was ended, as they were returning, the boy Jesus stayed behind in Jerusalem. His parents did not know it, but supposing Him to be in the company they went a day's journey, and they sought Him among their kinsfolk and acquaintances; and when they did not find Him, they returned to Jerusalem, seeking Him. After three days they found Him in the temple, sitting among the teachers, listening to them and asking them questions; and all who heard Him were amazed at His understanding and His answers. And when they saw Him they were astonished; and His mother said to Him, 'Son, why hast Thou treated us so? Behold, Thy father and I have been looking for Thee anxiously.' And He said to them, 'How is it that you sought Me? Did you not know that I must be in My Father's house?' And they did not understand the saying which He spoke to them. And He went down with them and came to Nazareth, and was obedient to them; and His mother kept all these things in her heart.

LUKE ii. 41–51

ON JESUS AT TWELVE YEARS OLD

CHAPTER ONE

CHRIST'S THREE DAYS IN JERUSALEM

IT is your wish, my dearest son, that I should read and study that part of the Gospel which tells us about the things which Jesus did when He was a young boy of twelve.[1] And you want me to send you letters containing the seeds, as it were, of meditation and love which grew out of my reading. Believe me when I say that, even while your messenger was telling me of this request of yours, I realized at once what great love and burning devotion to our Lord, had brought you to ask this favour of me, dearest of brothers. Then suddenly there came back to my mind the feelings and reactions I used to experience whenever I heard that Gospel read or sung. But it is no longer like that any more, for I can see how far behind I have left such sweet thoughts and blissful feelings. How far the ties of worldly cares and secular business have drawn me from those delights! Now I am poor and wretched, and I have to feed on things which my soul then would not even touch.[2] When I remember those delights of long ago, my heart breaks within me,[3] and I think of how the Lord stretched out His hand and touched my heart, anointing it with His mercy and lovingkindness.

So you can see quite easily how your love and devotion make a beautiful and glorious light shine on me through your request that I should try to tell you where Jesus was during those three days when His mother searched every-

where for Him. Where did He lodge? What food did He
eat? Whose company did He enjoy? What affairs busied
Him so much? These are the sort of things you are wonder-
ing about. And I know well, my son, that these are the
same questions you put to Jesus Himself in your prayers.
With great intimacy and love-longing, even with tears, you
beg Him to answer you whenever the picture of that dear
child comes before your eyes. And when your imagination
conjures up His beautiful face; when you feel those eyes of
His meek and loving, happily gazing on you, your deep
love and unsatisfied longing force you to cry out: O sweet
child, where wast Thou? Where didst Thou hide? What
shelter didst Thou have? What delightful company didst
Thou have? Was it in heaven or on earth? Didst Thou
stay in some house during those days, or didst Thou go to
some hiding place with a few boys of Thine own age, and
there tell them the mysteries of God and the secrets of
heaven? Didst Thou thus obey the command given by
Thee in the Gospel: 'Let the children come to Me, and do
not hinder them.'⁴ O they were happy indeed who lived
in close intimacy with Thee, if any there were, and who
enjoyed Thy presence for those three days.

   But why, sweetest Lord, didst Thou show no pity
towards Thy mother who sought Thee with such tears and
sorrow? For Thy mother and father were searching for
Thee everywhere, and yet Thou wouldst not comfort them.
And why, dear Lady, didst thou seek after thy Son when
thou knewest quite well that He was God? Wast thou
afraid that hunger and cold would worry Him, or that He
would come to any harm from boys of His own age?
Didst thou not remember that He was God, that He feeds
and cares for all creatures and things, and clothes with more
glory than the great king Solomon, that grass of the fields
which lives to-day and will feed the oven to-morrow?⁵

And how was it that thou didst lose Him so easily? Why—it is by thy leave that I ask such bold questions—why wast thou so unwatchful that thou didst not notice His disappearance until it was too late? Jesus has told me what He replied to His mother, in words which she alone could understand when she found Him after searching with such a burning love. And so I can write and tell you, my dearest brother, what He told me, and I can speak of things which I have tasted from His own lips.

CHAPTER TWO

THE CHILDHOOD OF JESUS

AND now, if you like, let us examine what happened before the event of which we are speaking. Jesus was born in Bethlehem, and when He was but a few days old, He was forced to hide in Egypt. Then after the death of Herod, He grew up in Nazareth. It was from there that He went up, not alone, but in His parents' care, to the temple in the capital of the land. But why did He do all this? Because He wanted us to see that He is our leader in life, the teacher of the way to heaven, and the healer of our pains and sickness. Surely He is our leader, for it is His joy and delight to run the course before us like an athlete, as the Psalmist says, starting from heaven[6] and coming down to Bethlehem. The perfume from His robes of majesty lingered behind Him there, while He hid in darkness,[7] as David puts it, in Egypt. And when He had flooded those who sat in darkness and deathly gloom[8] with the light of His heavenly grace, He went to Nazareth which became a great and famous city because it was His home. From Nazareth He came to Jerusalem and went into the temple, not to teach (although He was God), but to learn and listen to the doctors' teaching, and to ask questions. And during all this time He was in the care of His parents, and was obedient to them.

This is how Thou dost run the course before us, O Lord, teaching us the way and healing our infirmities. Thy example shows wanderers the right path; it affords a ladder to make it easy for those who are already mounting up to God. It makes the way of return clear to those who are exiles from the land of grace. O who will give me the strength and grace which I need to follow closely in Thy footsteps, O good Jesus, and so to run after Thee and clasp Thee at length in an embrace? For I am a prodigal son, who took the portion of the estate which was due to him.[9] I was selfish and would render nought to Thee. I set out for a distant land, a place where men have lost the likeness of God, and I became like the senseless beasts[10] through wasting my fortune in riotous living. At last I found I was in want, for there was no longer any bread for me to eat, and the husks which the swine used to eat did not avail to satisfy my hunger. Behind a herd of unclean animals I wandered, in a wilderness where there was no water,[11] and where no path was to be found leading to a town. My courage melted away in my plight, and I said: 'How many hired servants there are in my Father's house who have more bread than they can eat, and here am I perishing with hunger!'[12] When I cried out in these words, God heard me and led me by a straight road into a town of many people[13] —none other than the town where there is more than enough food; the town called 'House of Bread,' or in Hebrew 'Bethlehem.' May Thy mercy and kindness give glory to Thee, O Lord,[14] for Thou hast satisfied my starving soul, and in my hunger Thou hast filled my soul with good things. And this is because our Lord is the Bread which came down from heaven,[15] and was placed in a manger at Bethlehem. He became Bread to feed us who are but beasts in spirit.

CHAPTER THREE

THE CHILDHOOD OF THE SOUL

THIS is where, like a kind of spiritual birth, our conversion begins. And we begin to turn back to God, to be moulded by grace into the image of that little child, and to take up the banner of poverty as we follow Him. Like the dumb beasts[16] we stand before Thee, O Lord, drinking deep of the delights that flow from Thy presence. But yet we must not forget that grave warning of the scriptures: 'My son, if thy mind is to enter the Lord's service, wait there in His presence and prepare thyself to be put to the test.'[17] And our Lord does test us. For He hides His face from us for a little while. He does not mean to leave us completely, but only to hide from us. And when He does this, we are cast back into the land of Egypt, surrounded by darkness and confusion. There we lie in darkness,[18] overcast with the shadow of death, while the joy which we have tasted and now lost, makes our sufferings more bitter. Bonds of iron, shackles forged by the hardness of our hearts, hold us so that we are helpless to escape.

What can we do when we are in such trouble, but cry out to the Lord our God? Straightway He delivers us from our distress, flooding with the brightness of His consolation the darkness of temptation which surrounds us. And the fetters of our hardheartedness He shatters with the grace which He pours into our troubled souls. Then, because we have triumphed in the test, our Lord is joyful. He leads us to Nazareth, where the scriptures flower. And there our food is the fruit of virtue, when we are subject to those who have charge over us. It is in this way that we enjoy the same delights as Jesus did when He was twelve years old. For just as He is conceived and born in us,[19] so too does He grow up in us, until we reach perfect manhood and maturity, when His growth in us is complete.

CHAPTER FOUR

THE JOY OF CHRIST'S COMPANIONSHIP

'AND when Jesus was twelve years old, after going up to Jerusalem as the custom was at the time of the feast, and completing the days of its observance, His parents set about their return home. But the boy Jesus continued His stay in Jerusalem.' Now, so that none of the beauty of this incident may escape us, we must not forget that it was a Jewish custom for the men and women to go up to the feast day separately. This was meant to ensure that nothing defiled should even draw near to the celebrations of the feast, for it was laid down in the law that only those who were clean should take part in the sacred rites. And so we can understand more easily that Jesus granted His sweet presence now to His father and the company of the men, now to His mother and the women who journeyed to Jerusalem with her.

Let us, then, try to imagine the happiness of those who had the privilege of seeing that beautiful face of His during the days of that journey, and of hearing His words, sweet with the mysteries of God. They saw heavenly grace and power shining in Him, and heard Him tell of the secrets of life-giving wisdom. The old men in the company are amazed at Him, and the younger men are filled with wonder because they have never seen such a boy before. Such mature behaviour in a boy of His age, and words so full of import from one so young, make them all a little afraid. And I am sure that His beautiful face shone with such heavenly grace and power that all eyes were turned towards Him. And the ears of them all strained to catch every word from His lips. For He drew everyone there to Himself by inflaming them with love. See how they grasp Him! The old men caress Him. The young ones clasp Him in an embrace. The children follow Him about as if they were His slaves. What tears they shed when the old men keep Him in their company too long! How the holy women complain when He lingers with His father and the men who crowd around Him! I believe that each and every one cried out that day with fondest longing: 'O that he would kiss me with the kisses of his mouth!'[20] And sometimes when those of His own age yearned to be with Him, they did not dare to intrude upon the discussions which the old men so delighted to have with Him. And it must have seemed as if the words in the Canticle had been written specially for them: 'O that thou wert like a brother to me, that nursed at my mother's breast! If I met thee outside, I would kiss thee, and none would despise me.'[21]

Share their joy, I beg you, as they enter the holy city, and see how each and every part of that company strives to have Him and enjoy His presence before the others. How truly happy is he who succeeds! And perhaps it was for this reason that, when the observance of the feast-day was over, and the company set about their return home, the boy Jesus, unknown to His parents, continued His stay in Jerusalem. For His mother thought He was with His father, so much was He loved and sought after by all those who journeyed with them. And since His parents did not realize that He was missing, it was not until they had gone a whole day's journey that they searched for Him among the throng which had gone up to the city at the same time as they had. So they made inquiry for Him among their kinsfolk and acquaintances, as Saint Luke tells us. And when they could not find Him, they made their way back to Jerusalem to search for Him there.

But it was only after three days that they found Him in the temple. Where wast Thou during those three days, O good Jesus? Who gave Thee food and drink, or a bed to sleep on? Who had the great privilege of untying the straps of Thy shoes, for even John the Baptist thought himself unworthy of doing that? Or who was allowed to prepare baths and oils for Thy boyish limbs? Sweetest Lord, I do not know the answers to any of these questions, but I do know that, just as it was of Thy own will that Thou didst take on Thyself our weakness and uselessness, so couldst Thou show that Thou wast all-powerful too. And so, during those three days, Thou wast in no way bound to experience the neediness of that human nature which Thou hadst taken upon Thyself. But still I ask, where wast Thou, O Lord Jesus? There is no definite answer we can find to this question, and so we may not lay anything down as certain. But we may guess or imagine anything we like. What shall I say, Lord God? I could say that Thou didst go about begging from door to door, for in this way Thou wouldst have shared completely in our poverty, and taken on Thyself all the lowliness of our human nature. Oh, who will give me some of those scraps of food? And then I can share in His begging, or at least eat the crumbs and remnants of what my God has eaten!

CHAPTER FIVE

THE THREE DAYS OF OUR REDEMPTION

LET us look now at the secrets of the first day that Jesus spent alone in Jerusalem, because by looking into them we shall come to an understanding of mysteries with an even deeper meaning. On the first day, then, Jesus appeared before His Father. He did not come into His Father's presence to take the seat at His right hand, and reign with Him in majesty, but He came to ask His Father what He wished Him to do. And God the Son had to do this because He had come down from heaven and taken our human nature with all its weaknesses and frailties except sin. Now, although we cannot say for certain what the boy Jesus did when He stayed behind in Jerusalem, this opinion is not entirely absurd if we remember that the Son of God, being equal with the Father and the Holy Spirit, and sharing in the divine nature with Them, disposed and ordered all things from the beginning. But He had taken upon Himself the nature of a slave, as Saint Paul tells us,[22] and so man asked God what He willed for him, and a lowly creature sought to know the wishes of the Most High. But, as we have just said, the Son of God did not really seek to know what He had known as God from all eternity; He wished merely to submit Himself to the Father in all things, and to be entirely obedient and humble before the will of God.

All had been foreseen by the Father . . . Our Lord's baptism, the choosing of the disciples, and the composing of the gospels. The inscrutable will of God had decided that the Son of Man would perform miracles and die in cruel suffering, only to rise again in glory from the grave.

Then, after appearing before His Father and submitting
Himself to the Father's will, the sweetness of the face of
Jesus made the angels and archangels sing for joy on the
second day. With them the whole of heaven rejoiced, for
by His death Jesus would soon rebuild the ruins which the
wicked and rebellious spirits left when they were cast down
to hell. Then the Patriarchs and Prophets saw Him on the
third day when He mingled with them, His presence prov-
ing what they had heard but a short time before from holy
Simeon. And in this way He soothed their longing hearts,
filling them all with joyful expectation of His coming in
triumph to open the gates of heaven to all.

It was therefore quite fitting that He should be found in
the temple on the third day, sitting among the elders and
teachers, after the Patriarchs and Prophets had heard Him
proclaim the Father's plan for the redemption of mankind.
So it was that in the holy temple in Jerusalem, He began to
unfold the secrets of heaven to those who were learned in
the scriptures, for therein lies the priceless treasure of the
promise of God's mercy. But He did not open that treasure
house to them all at once, but gradually. At first He listened
to them and asked them questions, and then He addressed
them openly. 'And all those who heard Him were in
amazement at His quick understanding and at the answers
He gave.'[23] Now this model of humility is shown here in
our Lord, so that those who are young may see how they
should be silent before those who are old and wise. If they
will listen and ask questions, they can learn great things.

But now, dearest Lady and mother of my Lord, tell me
something of what thou didst feel when thou didst find thy
Son talking to the teachers of the law, instead of playing
with boys of His own age as thou didst expect. What joy,
what amazement thou must have felt, when thou sawest all
eyes fixed on Him, and everyone eager to catch every word

He uttered! Everyone without exception, great and lowly, learned and unlettered, remarked upon His quick understanding and the answers He gave. Didst thou sing, like the bride in the Canticle, 'I found him whom my soul loves. I held him and would not let him go'?[24] Yes, sweet mother, clasp Him whom thou lovest so dearly. Kiss and embrace Him, putting thine arms about His neck, and recapture those three lost days by enjoying anew the sweetness of His presence.

Yet I hear thee asking: 'My son, why hast thou treated us so? Think what anguish of mind Thy father and I have endured, searching for Thee!'[25] When I hear this question I cannot help asking thee again, why wast thou so sad, my Lady? For it is my opinion that thou wast not filled with any sort of fear for the boy whom thou didst know to be God. Thou wast not afraid that He would suffer from hunger or thirst. No, thy search was not so much motivated by fear, as by the yearning to taste those unspeakable delights of His presence which thou hadst lost for even such a little time as three days. And this I can readily understand, for I know how sweet my Jesus is to those who taste Him, how beautiful He is to those who see His face, and how tender He is to those who embrace Him. What great sorrow must we feel, then, if He leaves us for even a moment!

CHAPTER SIX

THE WISDOM OF MARY AND JESUS

'But what reason had you to search for me? Could you not tell that I must needs be in my Father's house?'[26] In these words He begins to unveil to us the innermost meaning of those hidden things of heaven which had been His concern during those last three days. And after His parents had found Him and questioned Him, He gave us an outstanding example of humility and obedience, and of how to give up our own will. He shows us, too, how we must do what we are told to do by those who have charge over us, even if it means leaving undone things that we think are very useful and important. For He gave up many things which were of great importance, putting His parents' wishes before His own, and going down with them on their journey back to Nazareth. 'And He lived there in subjection to them.'[27]

But what else do we read in the gospel? It is this: 'These words which He spoke to them were beyond their understanding.' Now I do not think that what Saint Luke says here refers to Mary, for, since the Holy Ghost came down on her, and the power of the Most High overshadowed her,[28] she must have known the real reason for everything her Son did. The gospel is speaking, I think, of those who could not have known or understood the meaning of Jesus' question, while Mary, who did know, 'kept in her heart the memory of all this.'[29] For she remembered this event in its entirety, and thought about it frequently, keeping it safe in her heart with all the other things she had seen and heard about her Son. And our mother was looking after us when she kept safe the memory of all this, for she feared that her Son's words might slip by without notice. Then they would neither be written in the gospel nor be spread by His disciples, and those who eat the heavenly bread of His word with such joy would be deprived of the delight they have in tasting every one of His sayings. And so she kept this in her heart, guarding it for us, and telling no one, until she saw that the time was ripe to tell it to the apostles and disciples, for them to preach to all nations.

'And so Jesus advanced in wisdom with the years, and in favour both with God and with man.'[30] There has been much discussion about the meaning of these words, yet no two opinions are the same. But we shall not linger over judging these various views and theories because that is not our purpose here. One theory is that Christ's wisdom was equal to God's, since His soul was created and taken up into the Godhead. And there are some who are afraid of making a creature equal to the Creator, and so they say that, as Jesus grew up His wisdom increased, relying on the gospel to support their view. 'Jesus advanced in wisdom with the years.' No wonder, they claim, that Christ's wisdom was less than God's, for He could suffer and die, whereas God cannot. They conclude then, that Christ did not enjoy the same happiness and beatitude as the Father.[31]

As far as I am concerned, anyone can think what he likes about these opinions, but it is enough for me to know and believe that our Lord Jesus was perfect God, since He was and always will be one of the three persons in the Godhead. And since this is so, His wisdom was all-knowing, His justness was without flaw. He shared in God's unmarred beatitude, and His power could do all things. He was, is, and will be all-perfect. And so I have no doubt at all that whatever we can say of God in His Godhead, could have been said of Christ too, even when He was yet unborn in

His mother's womb. We must say also that Christ, until He had triumphed at His resurrection, could suffer and die like any other man, because He was a man, not just by outward appearance but by nature, and so He could grow with the years. But did He grow in wisdom also? I leave this for those to discuss among themselves who revel in arguing about such things.

CHAPTER SEVEN

GROWING UP IN SPIRIT

BUT you did not ask me for theories and arguments, dearest son. You want my words to bring you the beginnings of devotion to raise your mind to God. You have no use for those twists of speech which come from quick wits. So let us then leave out the unimportant historical details, and try to come to some really deep understanding of the spiritual meaning of this event in our Lord's life, asking Him to give us grace and guidance in what we say. The Lord our God is one God. He cannot be changed or swayed. 'Thou art the same and thy years have no end.'[32] It is in these words that David tells us how God is eternal, timeless, unchangeable. But when He took our human nature He became subject to change and the rigours of time, so that He could open a road for us to His timelessness and changelessness. It is because He did this that we find in our Saviour the way for our climb towards God, Who is the life to which we hope and long to come, and the truth which we shall enjoy in the delight of heaven, as He Himself tells us: 'I am the way and the truth and the life.'[33] It is the Lord of all Who is changeless; yet it was the Lord of all Who took our flesh upon Himself, and was born in Bethlehem.

With the passing of time, our Lord grew up, as all children grow, so that we who are such little ones in mind and spirit—indeed, we are less, we are almost nothing— might be born again in spirit and pass through all the stages of spiritual growth and development. Thus, when He grows in stature, we develop spiritually, and whatever He

does throughout His life on earth, is done also in the souls
of those of us who pass steadily and successfully through the
various stages of progress in holiness. Let us then take His
birth into this world as the model for our own spiritual
birth, our turning back to God. And the persecution which
Herod turned against Him when He was but a few days old,
is a warning that we shall have to suffer temptations from
Satan when we first tear ourselves from the things of this
world and give ourselves to the things of God. And the
years that He spent growing up in Nazareth show us how
we must grow in goodness and virtue.

You remember how the prodigal son, when he was weak
with hunger, was invited into the house, where there was
bread in plenty.[34] And let us remember, too, that Bethlehem
means 'house of bread.' But there it is not bread of the
finest quality that he finds, but coarse loaves baked among
the ashes. And he undergoes the suffering of which the
psalmist warns him: ashes are to be his only food, and his
drink is to be nothing but what comes to him mingled with
his tears.[35] For later, in his father's house, he will eat a very
different kind of bread, made of the finest, purest wheat.
No ash from the hearth clings to its crust; no coarse grain
is in its fine texture, for it is pure and unleavened. What
can this bread be but the Word of God? 'In the beginning
was the Word, and the Word was with God, and the Word
was God.'[36]

But who, you may well ask, is worthy to eat such bread?
It is the bread of angels, who can taste it with all its savour
and see how sweet the Lord is, for their senses are perfect
and they know what true sweetness is. Although they are
angels, their teeth are still set on edge by sour grapes. But
so that man, too, might eat this food, the bread of angels
became man. He took on Himself the chaff of our lowliness
and uselessness. He sank Himself into the ashes from which

we are made and to which we must return. He mixed the leaven of our weakness with the purity of His divine nature. It was in this way that the bread of angels became man, the all-powerful became small and puny, and He Who holds all in His hand became poor. But why did He do all these things? So that you who are so great in your own eyes may follow His example of humility, and become little and insignificant like Him; so that you, with all your riches and lust for gain, may become poor like Him by casting aside your wealth and abundance. There will be no room for you in the inn either,[37] in the land of spiritual birth, for worldly company will cast you out. Your own wishes and feelings can hold no sway over you. You must rely in all obedience on someone else's judgement, not on your own wits and efforts. Ashes from the hearth will encrust the bread you eat, when the Lord allots you nothing but tears for your daily food and drink.[38]

This is what you will find when you are born in Christ, and Christ is born in you. What alarm fills Herod's heart— by Herod I mean the devil—when Christ trespasses on his domain! He cannot but be angered when he sees how his home has become Christ's dwelling-place. In revenge his sword flashes bright,[39] he bends his bow in readiness; and deadly are the weapons he fits to it before shooting at the upright of heart from the darkness of his hiding-place.[40] The flesh he inflames with lustful desires. Wicked thoughts set the peaceful mind in a turmoil. All sweetness is drained from the souls of Christ's newborn children, and they are assailed by a different temptation wherever they turn. Then it is that you think that Christ has deserted you, but when Herod has himself been put to the sword by the grace of God's mercy and pity, and not by your own efforts, Christ returns, bringing a new and deeper peacefulness.

Now that Herod is dead, Christ waits for you to begin

your journey to Nazareth, for after temptation you must
make haste to climb up to the practice of virtue, just as our
Lord came up from Egypt to Nazareth after those who
sought His life were dead. Now you know that Nazareth
is the Hebrew for 'city of flowers.' But although fruit
results from flowers, flowers and fruits are not the same
thing. So, too, these spiritual endeavours and exercises are
not virtues in themselves, although with God's grace and
help they lead to virtue and goodness. And so, while we
are in Nazareth, we must produce not only spiritual flowers
but spiritual fruits as well. From there, when the time is
ripe, we must journey on to Jerusalem.

CHAPTER EIGHT

THREE DAYS IN THE HISTORY OF ISRAEL

WHEN He was twelve years old, Jesus too went up to Jerusalem. Now this journey has a meaning which may not be apparent to you: Christ left the synagogue at Nazareth to come into the church of the Gentiles, and to show His presence on earth. He was twelve years old at the time, and that was a very fitting age for Him to leave Nazareth for Jerusalem, as I shall explain. He had not come on earth to set aside the law, but to bring it to perfection. And therefore He added to the ten commandments given to Moses in the Old Testament the two commandments of the New Testament which we must keep if we would be perfect: 'Thou shalt love the Lord thy God with thy whole heart and thy whole soul and thy whole mind. Thou shalt love thy neighbour as thyself.'[41] There are few words in this twofold law of charity, but yet it sums up everything that we must do, and it brings the law and the prophets to perfection.

And so the boy Jesus, unbeknown to His parents, continued His stay in Jerusalem.[42] Yes, even to this day Christ is in the temple which is His church, but the Jews, who are His parents by race, do not realize it. Joseph is still in Egypt, and it is the Egyptians, not the Jews, who call Him the Saviour of the world.[43] For while He is distributing fine wheat to the Egyptians, who are Gentiles, His own brethren are perishing for want of the Word of God, among the unclean spirits of the land of Canaan. 'His parents thought He was among their travelling companions,'[44] Saint Luke explains. But why should they go on thinking that even

now? Do you still think, sons of Israel, that Christ keeps
company with you, when your own prophet Jeremiah tells
you quite plainly that He has forsaken His home, and has
done with His chosen people?[45] 'My heritage has become
to me like a lion in the forest. She has lifted up her voice
against me; therefore I hate her.'

What signs have you seen, what marks of grace does He
bestow on you, that you should even imagine that He is
still with you? What has happened to the temple now?
Where are the daily sacrifices and the priests to offer them?
What has become of that altar which stood in Jerusalem?
Does the ever-burning fire still flame? When it dies, how
can there be burnt sacrifices, since they may be offered on
no other hearth? Either these things are no longer yours,
or you have them against God's command. And therefore,
you do not have Christ. In days gone by you did have
Christ, for every event of the Old Testament foreshadowed
His coming. But when He did come, types and prophecies
had no more significance. Yet you still rely on them, and
look out for their fulfilment, although your waiting will be
in vain. How you persist in your errors! How blind you
are to the things about you!

No, the Jews do not see how the prophecies have been
fulfilled, and the law brought to perfection. Still they think
that He is with them, as they seek Him among their kinsfolk
and acquaintances. Whom are you looking for, sons of
Juda? From the mountainside has already fallen that stone
no hand had quarried,[46] and do you still go on searching?
Scattered as you are throughout the world, you sin against
Christ wherever you go, and still you do not see Him.
Your Amen rises up from the lands of every nation to give
praise to God and His Anointed; you sing Alleluia to God
the Father and God the Son, your Hosanna rings out to
your Creator and Redeemer. What need have you to

search further? Where the sun is, there He takes up His
abode, so that no one may escape from its burning heat.[47]
Why, then, do you turn and look elsewhere?

But do you really seek Him among your kinsfolk and
acquaintances? For if you look in Isaiah you will read:
'The ox knows its owner and the ass its master's crib. But
Israel does not know; my people does not understand.'[48]
How, then, can you hope to find Him? And if you ask
David, he will tell you that your feast has turned into a
trap, a snare to recoil on you. 'Ever the blind eye is yours,
and the bowed back.'[49] If you are so blind you will never
see Him. When you look again, and search in Jeremiah,
you read: 'The priests did not say "where is the Lord?"
Those who handle the law did not know me.'[50] What the
prophet says proves that you cannot hope to find Him.
Then you turn to the book of Moses, but to this day, when
Moses is read out a veil hangs over your hearts,[51] and so
you are condemned to go on seeking.

CHAPTER NINE

CHRIST'S JOURNEY TO JERUSALEM

'Return, return, O Shulammite'[52] to Jerusalem, and you will find Him. You can read how, when someone told Jesus that His mother and His brethren were waiting for Him outside the house,[53] He did not go out to see them. And why does He not come out to meet you now? Because you must go in yourselves, and then your search will be ended. 'They made their way back to Jerusalem,' the gospel tells us, 'and it was only after three days that they found Him.' But Isaiah tells us that only a remnant of Jacob will turn back to God,[54] the Mighty One, countless though Israel be, as the sea sand. But when will they turn back to God? Surely, it will be after three days—a time we must long for with all our hearts.

When, oh when will Israel come back to the Lord their God, and fear their king, David?[55] When will they all accept one ruler and come up out of the land of darkness? O good, sweet Jesus, when will this be? When wilt Thou look in mercy on Thine own people and family,[56] for it is unheard of that a man should bear ill will to his own flesh and blood? Then share Thy bread with the hungry,[57] O Lord, and give those poor wanderers a welcome to Thy house. How long must Cain wander in wretchedness and misery, flying from his fellow men?[58] How long must he travel over that very earth which opened its mouth and received from his hand the blood which Thou didst shed in dying for us like another Abel? Hast Thou not already poured sevenfold retribution into his lap,[59] when everywhere the elder serves the younger;[60] when the yoke of oppression bears down on them wherever they go, and the sword of persecution is turned on them in every place? Is there none to rescue them, none to bring them help? In the end they will come back, I know, like the dogs who go scavenging about the cities,[61] and they will be faint with hunger for the word of God. But that will not be till day is drawing to its close, for 'it was only after three days that they found Him in the temple.'

Now when Jesus went into our Jerusalem, the Church, He hid on the first day from the Jews who were His brethren, and from the Synagogue that had mothered Him. Instead He preached to the Gentiles, just as the apostles were to do after His death. Why they did so was explained to the Jews by Saint Paul: 'Since you declare yourselves unfit for eternal life, we have turned our attention to the Gentiles.'[62] And it was the hearts of the Gentiles that were flooded with the light of heaven when our Lord taught in the temple on the first day. Banishing the mist and darkness of their former faithlessness, their new-found gift of faith pours its brightness into the minds of those who were once deemed lost and condemned to darkness for evermore. But the joyous light of day is overclouded by the darkness of persecution, for the princes of this world are filled with hatred and anger against Christ's followers. They order crosses and racks and fetters and wild beasts, and every conceivable kind of torture to be made ready, in order to stamp out the Christians and their hated religion. Although most of Christ's children overcame these tortures by the strength of their faith, many gave way and were mourned with great sorrow by the saints. But day always follows night, and the brightness of God's mercy and pity banishes the darkness of hatred and persecution.

On the second day then, the rulers are converted to Christ, and they throw down the heathen temples, and consecrate to the memory of the martyrs, shrines which were formerly used for the worship of demons. Little by little, as the truth of the Holy Spirit permeates men's hearts, the night of faithlessness and Godlessness is routed. But again a shadow is cast on this shining day by the cloud of heresy. The error is brought to light by the doctors of the Church, who are tireless in their efforts to preserve the faith which they have pondered for so long. And as the cloud of heresy leaves the hearts of Christ's followers, the sun of righteousness beams down again on a world freed from fatal danger.

But even now, evening is falling and the third day is nearly done.[63] Dreadful perils come upon us with that dusk, for the light of the third day is put to flight by the abandoned life of false Christians whose wickedness enshrouds a fast ageing world. Love grows cold in the hearts of men,[64] as they see wickedness at large, while we long for the dawning of that day when His mother, the Synagogue, will find Jesus at last, as the stories of Enoch and Elijah show she will. For surely it is after she has entered that temple which is the church, that she will find Him as He sits there among the elders and doctors, the Mediator between God and men.[65] And as Jesus Christ, true God and true man, sits there, He is an example to us all. As He listens, He shows young children how they must be attentive to God's word. His questions show young people how they must inquire diligently into the truths of their faith. He shows those who are older how they must spread God's message to men, just as He, although only twelve years old at the time, gave instruction to the elders and doctors in Jerusalem.

CHAPTER TEN

ISRAEL'S SEARCH FOR GOD

YES, the house of Jacob will echo with shouts of gladness and rejoicing, when the Jewish people recognize the true Joseph at the end of the world, and hear the news that He is still alive, just as was told to Jacob long ago: 'Your son Joseph is still alive, and he is ruler over all the land of Egypt.'[66] But when they hear this good news, every tongue will ask the question that our Lady asked: 'Son, why hast Thou treated us so? Think what anguish of mind Thy father and I have endured, searching for Thee.'[67] Why, then, didst Thou treat them so, Joseph, son of Jacob? Thy mother is dead, and endless grief crushes Thy father at her loss and Thine. Distress surrounds Thy brethren on all sides. Great hardship and unhappiness bear down on Thy birthplace. How canst Thou, then, turn away from Thine own people and guide the Egyptians along the way of salvation? 'Why didst Thou treat us like this?' Thy brethren go into Egypt to search for food, and then return to their own land. And although they see that Thou art Lord of the earth, they do not recognize Thy face. That face, so unsurpassed in beauty, that the whole of Egypt gazes on with wonder, is concealed from Thine own kith and kin.

'Why hast Thou treated us so?' Thou dost look on Thine own family as strangers, accusing them of evil and threatening to punish them, for although Thou art merciful and kind to everyone else, Thine own people find Thee harsh and cruel. 'Why didst Thou treat us like this?' The prodigal son Thou didst tell of, swallowed up his patrimony[68] in the company of harlots. He gave himself to lovers of wood and stone,[69] and exchanged the glory of the imperishable God for representations of man and bird, beast and reptile.[70] And when he returned to his father's house after spending many years away from home, he was given the flesh of a fatted calf to eat, and the purest blood of fine grapes to drink. He ate and made merry amid music and dancing. But what happens to the children of Israel? They stand outside like strangers,[71] although the covenant, the giving of the law, the temple worship and the promises belong to them, and although theirs is the human stock from which the Saviour came. Only a new miracle can rebuild the temple and restore its priesthood, bringing the scattered sons of Israel back to the Jerusalem that they love so dearly. At last they will find Christ in their own land of Juda, and will no longer worship in the woodland plains.[72]

'We have been looking for Thee in great distress,' the Blessed Virgin said. Great, too, has been the distress of Israel, for the miracles and wonders of days gone by are shown to them no longer. The voices of the prophets are heard no more, and no holy oil anoints the king and the high priest. All these things bore witness to Thy coming, O Lord, and so Israel could not believe that Thou hadst gone to grace another dwelling with Thy presence. They never thought that Thou, Who wast God's gift and promise to them, hadst left Thy chosen and favoured race in order to go to the salvation of rival nations. They never understood how it could have happened that Thou didst prefer the Gentiles, unclean with the worship of false gods and idols, to Thy one-time favourites. It was for Israel that the sea rolled back;[73] for Israel that manna came down from heaven.[74] It was Israel's thirst that was slaked with water from the rock. It was the children of Israel who went into the midst of the sea, between the walls of water. It was for them, too, that the walls of Jericho fell down.[75] For them

the sun stood still and the moon stayed its course. And
although Thou hast done all these things for Israel, Thou
hast left them for the Gentiles.

When Thy coming is proved to the Jews by countless
signs and miracles, they lose all hope, remembering how
Thou hast called the Gentiles and driven Thine own people
away. And so their search goes on. 'What reason had you
to search for Me?'[76] Christ asks when they complain to
Him. 'Could you not tell that I must be in My Father's
house?' . . . You are too slow of wit, too dull of heart, to
believe all those sayings of the prophets! Was it not fated
that Christ should suffer and then should come into His
glory, and that repentance and forgiveness of sins should be
preached in His name to all nations? Have you never heard
what the Father said to the Son? This is how David puts it:
'Ask Thy will of Me and Thou shalt have the nations for
Thy patrimony, the very ends of the world for Thy
domain.'[77] What reason, then, had you to search for Me?
Why did you not find Me at once among the Gentiles?
Did not Abraham receive this promise from God: 'All the
races of the world shall find a blessing through thy pos-
terity'?[78] Are you still unable to see that I must be about
My Father's business?

Listen, then, to what the Father says to Me in the book of
Isaiah: 'It is too light a thing that Thou shouldst be My
servant, to raise up the tribes of Jacob and to bring back
the poor remnant of Israel. I have appointed Thee to be
the light of the Gentiles. In Thee will I send out My salvation to the furthest corners of the earth.'[79] And did not
Jacob call Me 'the hope of all the nations,'[80] and Haggai say
that I am 'the prize which the whole world treasures'?[81]
Have you not read what Malachi said of Me: 'There is no
corner of the world, from sun's rise to sun's setting, where
My renown is not heard among the Gentiles, so revered is

My name among them'?[82] You begrudged My love and
mercy to all men, and you were afraid of My powers and
My gifts to mankind. And because you gazed enviously on
the salvation which was offered to those who did penance,
your spite and envy blinded you so that you could not see
the author of your own salvation. Therefore I have been
unforgiving with the branches that were native to the tree,
and I have cut them off from their natural root.[83] In their
place I have grafted branches from another stock. But now
I shall bestir Myself and give Zion redress,[84] for it is time
now to take pity on her. Those whom I had once cast off
I shall call back to My side, and gather into My embrace
the people I had scattered over the earth. I shall take into
My house again those whom I had driven out of My
company,[85] for you must all know that I am with you
every day, until the end of time.

CHAPTER ELEVEN

THE GIFTS OF THE SPIRIT

HAVING said something about the hidden meaning of our Lord's stay in Jerusalem, I feel it is high time for me to turn my attention to you, my dearest son, for it is your great wish to model yourself on Christ and to follow closely in His footsteps. So I hope I shall be able to draw on what is to be read in the Gospels, to explain to you the path you have to follow. Then you will be able to read in my pages what you experience happening within yourself. For I think you have already left the poverty of Bethlehem for the riches of Nazareth. Now that you are twelve years old in spirit, you have gone up from Nazareth with its flowers, to the fruits of Jerusalem, just as Jesus did at the same age. And when you have arrived at Jerusalem, you can see these heavenly truths being wrought in you just as you can read about them in a book.

Bethlehem was where Christ was born in poverty, and it is there that we begin our life of holiness. Nazareth is the place where Christ grew up, and there we begin to put our virtue and goodness to some effect. In the same way, Jerusalem, to which our Lord went up when He was twelve years old, is where we receive the grace to contemplate the secrets of heaven. In Bethlehem, then, the soul becomes poor by renouncing the world entirely, and in Nazareth it grows rich by bringing its virtue and goodness to perfection. Jerusalem is where the soul drinks deep of the sweetness of spiritual delights. Yet before we can come to the altar of contemplation, the soul must pass through the valley of tears, and journey across the rough lands of temptation, and the plains of spiritual endeavour. But before all else we must begin in Bethlehem, by giving over to God the infancy of our new way of life.

This kind of childhood has none of the quick, sharp wit of worldly men, and so it harms and deceives no one. Lusts and gainful desires have no place in it, and self-will is entirely alien to it. It passes judgement on no one and does not speak ill of any man. It is not greedy for possessions, since the opinions and judgements of another control all that it does. No care for the present, no worries about the future, can trouble this childhood, to which we are all encouraged by God's chosen instrument, Saint Paul, who tells us that 'if any one thinks that he is wise in this age, let him become a fool that he may become wise.'[86] And our Lord gives us this stern warning in the Gospel: 'Unless you turn and become like children, you will never enter the kingdom of heaven.'[87]

Now when a soul has become a little child, as Christ says it must, it will look forward to being twelve years old. But first it must suffer persecution from Herod, and during the seven years it spends in Nazareth, the city of flowers, virtue and goodness must blossom brightly in its rich soil. But before even this can happen, the field of our heart must be dressed and fertilized, and this is done by recalling our sins to mind, and considering our weakness and uselessness. Then it must be ploughed and harrowed by temptation, so that the seeds of goodness and virtue may bring forth flowers of spiritual endeavour. So when you see a man from whom the spirit of fear has cut out the old vices and deep-rooted lusts, you may say that he is spiritually a boy in his first year.

At the age of two, the spirit of piety will have made him meek and obedient. Next, the spirit of knowledge enters his soul, making him realize how weak he is without God's constant help, and so he comes to his third year. It is the spirit of strength that brings him to his fourth year, and you should look carefully at such a man, and see how strong and firm he has become against all those temptations and sensual pleasures which besiege his soul.[88] Discretion and discernment are the gifts of the spirit of counsel to the man who has reached his fifth year, and when he goes on to meditate on God's law, it is because the spirit of understanding has brought him safely to the age of six. Then, since widsom comes from meditation on the divine law, the spirit of wisdom follows, bringing him to his seventh year, and with this spirit come four more virtues and four more years. Nothing in life avails a man more than these four, as we read in Wisdom's own book: 'Temperance and prudence she teaches, with justice and fortitude, and what in life avails man more?'[89] Is is on these four that all the other virtues depend. Without them, you cannot have the rest. It is temperance that sees to it that our advance in these virtues is restrained and not excessive. Prudence ensures that we discern the qualities of each virtue distinctly, and in due order. The work of justice prevents us from using virtues in a disorderly and immoderate way, and it is fortitude that makes us determined to have and keep them always.

Then follows the twelfth year with its gift of the light of contemplation, when the spirit of the Lord rests on a man at last.[90] For it is the light of contemplation that conducts the yearning soul to the heavenly Jerusalem, and opens up the heavens and unlocks the gates of paradise. Then the soul which is spotless and pure sees its Spouse, fairer than all the children of men,[91] and it hears His voice as He gazes in at the window of the heart[92]: 'Thou art all fair my love; there is no flaw in thee.'[93] No stains of sin and passion mar its beauty. How could they when the soul has fled from the snares of all worldly thoughts and interests, when it has cast out the memories of days and deeds of long ago, and ceased to gaze on the world which clouded its vision of the Beloved.

When it hears its Spouse say those words, a burning desire wells up in its heart. As the soul raises its beautiful face to look more closely at Him Whom it loves, it hears again: 'Thou art all fair, my love, and thy lips distil nectar.[94] Lo, the winter is past, the rain is over and gone. The flowers appear on the earth.'[95] Now these flowers, although they have only just broken into bloom, are true virtues. As they spring up after the winter of persecution and the rains of temptation, they breathe forth a delightful fragrance. How Christ loves to see the beauty and breathe the sweet perfume of that man's heart, who has made great progress in holiness. Christ longs to possess that man's soul completely, and so He entices it to come to Him and leave worldly things for the things of God. 'For lo, the winter is past, the rain is over and gone. The flowers appear on the earth.' And now that the life of contemplating God has been opened to the soul, so that its cries of sorrow are heard no more, He adds . . . 'the voice of the turtledove is heard in our land.'

CHAPTER TWELVE

LOVE-LONGING FOR JESUS

REMEMBER too, my dearest son, how you talk to your Beloved, and how, like the pure dove which wanders alone, always sighing, you seek a place each day where you may be alone with your heart's love, although the noise and bustle of the world goes on about you. Never forget your longing sighs, your words to Him Whom your soul loves,[96] and the love which brings out in you the desire to see your lover. Sometimes you fret at the delays which keep you from Him, or claim that He is shunning you. Or sometimes you say that you are unworthy of His favours to you, but nevertheless, you take advantage of His goodness yet again. As you hang back, you try to force yourself forward by arguing with yourself, 'Why these tears, these sighs, these cries?' Your eyes are wet with tears as you gaze up to heaven, and your heart is heavy within you. You open your arms in supplication and then beat your breast and blame yourself for being so sluggish in spirit. Meanwhile, words without sense or meaning put forth in an endless torrent. They sometimes express your heartfelt desire, but often your longing overcomes you and your words become meaningless again.

Now our Lord is very happy when a soul overcomes Him at last. He loves to find a soul so urgent in its requests, and turns to the angels who stand about Him, and says: 'The voice of the turtledove is heard in our land.' Yes, the whole of heaven hears the voice of such a yearning soul, while the fragrance of its longing, wafting up to heaven, makes sweet the city of God. From what I have said you

will realize that you, too, must see what Elijah beheld in his
cave. 'A great strong wind passes by and rends the mountains and breaks the rocks, but the Lŏrd is not in that wind.
And after the wind comes an earthquake, but the Lord is
not in the earthquake. And after the earthquake comes a
fire, but the Lord is not in the fire. And after the fire comes
a still, small voice,'[97] and the Lord is in that voice. These
are the stages through which the soul must go up to God in
its prayer, just as a column of smoke rises up, all myrrh and
incense[98]—such sweet scents as the perfumer knows.

These things I put before you, not because I want you to
subject them to a close scrutiny and analysis, but because I
would have you attend carefully to see how they affect you
in your prayers. You should notice particularly how diffi-
cult it sometimes is, at first, for you to enter into your heart
to find a tomb in which to bury yourself amid the distractions of the world. Only then can you pray in secret,[99] as
our Lord says you must. And sometimes it seems as if a
great rock crushes your heart, and as if a huge mountain
blocks your heart's view of all spiritual things, until a great
strong wind passes by and rends the mountains and breaks
the rocks in pieces before the Lord. Then an earthquake
follows in the wake of this wind, when the soul, shaken by
remorse, bemoans the filth of sin which stains it. Moved by
sorrow for its sins, it purges out those stains. After the
earthquake, the heart is filled with hope, and the soul burns
with the fire of an unexpressible desire. We might almost
say that the soul fights with God to obtain its wish, until
a still, small voice silences its longing cries by calming its
restless thoughts and unchecked distractions. Then the soul
which contemplates God is carried up to the very gates of
the heavenly Jerusalem, where He looks lovingly on it Who
has been sought for so long, yearned for with such a burning

desire, and so often petitioned to put an end to the soul's exile.

He Who is fairer than all the children of men,[100] welcomes the soul to His arms. 'Arise, my love, my fair one, and come away.'[101] At the Lord's invitation, the soul goes into Jerusalem and passes into God's house, where He dwells in majesty, amid cries of joy and thanksgiving.[102] And the soul, clasped to the embrace of the Beloved, and covered with kisses, sings: 'I found Him whom my soul loves. I held Him and would not let Him go.'[103] Now it can give rein to its desires, enjoying the delight of the Beloved's presence, and celebrating a feast day with great rejoicing.[104]

When you are in this happy state, my dearest son, I beg you to remember me,[105] and when you come to where your King reigns in His sanctuary, ask Him to deliver me from this prison with its fetters and darkness. For I, too, would come once again into that freedom in which I formerly used to experience sich joy. And then I, too, will know what treasures of loving kindness the Lord stores up for those who fear Him.[106] But alas, such moments are few and far between! He is a truly happy man who can enjoy these delights for the length of three days—and by three days, I mean the threefold light of contemplation. For whatever the mind can know about God, when it has been enlightened by contemplation, must belong, either to God's power, or His wisdom, or His goodness.

CHAPTER THIRTEEN

THE THREEFOLD LIGHT OF
CONTEMPLATION

JESUS is mighty and strong in battle,[107] and if you really love Him, you may be sure that His right hand will protect you against all the powers of the world and the devil. For no one can resist Him; even the titanic powers obey Him.[108] Everything comes under His sway. All is dried up if He withholds the rain, and if He sends it, it floods all the earth. If, then, the strength of the evil one oppresses you, passions hurl their darts at you, the world turns upon you with hatred and persecution, and you are tempted to give up the life of holiness for very distaste, then you must run to Jesus. When dread and alarm fill your heart, so that at every second you are afraid that you will give way and be conquered, you must tell Jesus of the danger you are in, and how you need His help. Then He Whom you love will stay close to you, watching over you like a great king. He will take up shield and buckler,[109] as David once begged Him to do, and He will come to your help with the words: 'Be not afraid of them, for I am with you to deliver you.'[110]

Then, if you seek for wisdom, desiring to know the secrets of heaven, or to have some understanding of the chaotic state of this world, then look for Jesus in some secluded spot. When you can talk with Him quietly, put to Him those words of Jeremiah: 'Lord, I know well that right is on Thy side if I should complain to Thee, yet I must remonstrate with Thee.' For it may happen that you come near to turning away from God's path, when you see the good

fortune of sinners who defy His law,[111] who are not troubled
or stricken as other men are. 'Why is it,' you may ask, 'that
the affairs of the wicked prosper?'[112] But this, after all, is
the way in which our divine Master is wont to deal with
those who seek Him. He is indeed our Master, for it is He
Who teaches man all the wisdom that can be acquired.[113]
It is He Who opens our eyes to contemplate the wonders of
His law, and Who bears the key of knowledge. When He
opens the doors of wisdom, none may shut them, and when
He shuts them, none may open them.[114] In His right hand
He bears the law, like a flaming torch[115] wherewith to
enlighten us by the knowledge of God's commandments,
and to inflame us with that love which comes of pondering
the law. His left hand carries the sceptre of His kingship,[116]
a rod that rules with justice, and punishes the forwardness
of those who approach Him with presumption.

His power and His wisdom are wonderful, but if you
desire His goodness you will find that it is not enough to
receive but one kiss from Him; not enough to touch Him
but once, and to know only His lips. You will cry out and
complain with the prophet: 'It is Thy face that I seek, Lord,
and I long for Thy presence.'[117] You will sigh with the
bride in the Song of Songs: 'O that thou wert like a brother
to me, that nursed at my mother's breast! If I met thee
outside, I would kiss thee, and none would despise me.'[118]
Then He will certainly come to you, bringing with Him
the fragrance of rare perfumes.[119] He will kiss you so that
you thrill with an unspeakable joy, while He cries with
delight: 'Grace is bestowed upon thy lips.'[120]

There are many ways in which we may contemplate God
and see heavenly and spiritual things, but I believe that they
are all connected either with God's power, or His wisdom,
or His love and kindness. When you read the law and the
prophets you will find that certain figures and allusions

actually show how the soul contemplates God, and how God manifests Himself to those who love Him. For God is the cause of all things. It is His power which makes all things exist, and without Him nothing at all can have being. Some beings are possessed of reason, and through God's wisdom they, too, can attain wisdom, but without Him no teaching has any content. It is God's goodness that makes things good, and gives us the joy which we find in them. All things are safe with God, since nothing can rival His power. He makes everything sure and true, because His wisdom cannot be deceived. Who else but God can make things just and right, when no evil can stain or corrupt Him?

And so, when we think of the creation, it is God's power that strikes us most vividly. When we admire the nature of things we praise His wisdom. The use and enjoyment which we have from creatures is the gift of His love and kindness. But if you prefer to contemplate Him in what He did when He took upon Himself the nature of man, you will find it both easy and pleasant to watch how He shed brightness and light during the three days He spent alone in Jerusalem. When God's grace enlightens your mind so that you see the divine child lying in the manger, nestling in His mother's arms or feeding at her breast, or carried in the arms of Simeon in the temple—all this is the work of God's goodness that you see.

True, you must fear God's might and power when you remember how Christ's eyes flashed with anger and His voice thundered with rebuke, as He lashed the money-changers in the temple and threw over their tables, scattering all their money. Yet it is the light of His wisdom that will shine on you, when you see how He defeated the wiles of scribes and Pharisees with replies full of quick understanding and deep knowledge. You can see, too, that it was His power that put the demons to flight, and fed the crowds; it was His power that enabled Him to walk on the sea, and to call Lazarus from the tomb. It was His wisdom, and no foolishness, that inspired Him to deceive the devil by allowing Himself to be tempted, and by going hungry like a beggar. And in His wisdom He mounted the cross on which he was to die.

CHAPTER FOURTEEN

THE THREE DAYS OF CONTEMPLATION

IF it gives you great happiness and pleasure to think about
Christ's goodness and lovingkindness, go into the house of
Simon the Pharisee, and notice carefully what you see
there.[121] Look how tenderly, how gladly, how mercifully
He gazes at the sinful woman prostrate on the ground. See
with what pity and compassion He offers His feet to be
washed by the tears of this woman who begs forgiveness of
her sins, and to be wiped by that hair of hers which, until
now, pride and licentiousness have held in their possession.
See how lovingly and tenderly these feet are kissed by lips
which have formerly given witness of sinful loves. O happy
and holy sinner, kiss those beautiful feet of His! For it is
those feet which crush the serpent's head,[122] trampling on
sin and vice, and subduing the proud and mighty. At their
approach the old enemy takes to flight, and the hollow glory
of this world totters to destruction. Kiss His feet with those
lips which have at last found the kiss of joy and peace!

After hearing how you went to Him in Simon's house,
no sinner fears the approach of Christ. No man, however
dark his crimes, runs from the Lord. No one, however
unworthy, is filled with dread at His coming. Yes, kiss and
caress and wash those feet of Christ, which men and angels
must adore. Pour out the perfume of confession for your
sins, and let the whole house be fragrant[123] with your plea
for forgiveness. Woe to the Pharisee who is afraid that
another's sin may soil his house,[124] and who shuns the
perfume of Magdalen as if it were the smell of death. Your
own pride, Pharisee, stains you black and foul. How can

you know what a sweet scent Magdalen's misery was to the merciful Christ? You can have no idea of the great delight He found in her heartfelt sorrow. 'Her many sins have been forgiven her because she loved much': the fire of her love consumed her sin.

All the world must thank you, Mary Magdalen, because in the house of Simon the Pharisee it was you, happiest and holiest of sinners, who showed us all a safe haven for sinners. Where is that, if not at the feet of Jesus? For there, no one is scorned, no one is driven away, but everyone is received with welcome. As Jeremiah puts it, even an Ethiopian could turn white there,[125] or a leopard lose its spots; yet it is only the Pharisee who does not shed his cloak of pride at the feet of Jesus. Come, my soul, sinful and wretched, this is where you can shed your tears and wash away the stains of sinful kisses with the caress of penitence, while you pour out the oil of your love, safe from the temptations of those vices and sins which used to hold you in their grip. Why do you hang back, you floods of tears, when you should be flowing freely? No one will stop you, so wash the feet of my Lord, my Saviour and Protector. It does not matter to me if the Pharisee murmurs hard things against me in his heart, as Simon did,[126] nor if he thinks I should be barred from his house and banqueting hall. I do not mind at all if the Pharisee thinks I am unworthy to touch even the hem of Christ's garment,[127] or if he turns away to mock me, and to avoid hearing my cries. Whatever happens, I shall stay at Thy feet, O good Jesus, caressing them with my hands and pressing them to my lips. And I shall never stop washing them with my tears, and covering them with kisses, until I hear the words Thou didst say of the sinful woman: 'Her sins, which are many, are forgiven because her love was very great.'[128]

And so it is on the first day that a soul which thirsts for

God, the spring which satisfies all our longings and desires, lingers as it were in Jerusalem, where it gazes on its Maker and contemplates His divine power in great joy and happiness. His wisdom is the object of the soul's praise and wonder on the second day, while God in His love pours out goodness and sweetness on the third day, for the soul to taste with utmost contentment. For the first day gives the soul a vision of God's justice and righteousness which fill us with fear of His just judgements. And you would do well to remember what the prophet says about this: 'With the mighty deeds of the Lord God I will come. I will praise Thy righteousness, Thine alone.'[129] Then on the second day, the soul sees that knowledge which teaches all things, as we read in the psalms: 'And now in deep parables Thy wisdom has instructed me.'[130] And on the third day, the soul has a first glimpse of the divine mercy and goodness which pours blessings and favours on us all, and which we must value above all things, just as David did even when he was in the desert of Edom: 'To win Thy mercy, Lord, is dearer to me than life itself.'[131] So now you can see how fear, the result of pondering God's justice and righteousness, cleanses the soul of any stain or spot, while wisdom pours light into the heart on the second day. Then the soul receives a great gift when God's goodness and sweetness flood it with an unimaginable delight. But I am sure I would be wrong if I thought you did not understand how helpful, and even necessary, it is to indulge throughout the three days of your search for Jesus in the pleasures and delights which are to be found in Jerusalem. For there fear feeds you with the bread of sorrow, and knowledge gives you the wine of joy to drink, while goodness strengthens you with the milk of comfort and consolation.

Now although I have mentioned the delights of Jerusalem, you realize, I am sure, that sorrow is never far distant from them. For you have experienced how the soul prefers that sorrow which is the result of holy fear, to all the pleasures of this world—and here I also speak from experience. But those men whose merits are greater, whose minds are more brilliant, whose souls are purged more clean of the filth of sin and pride, are allowed to delve deeper into God's power and wisdom and goodness. There, in the divine power, they discover God's inscrutable judgements. In God's wisdom they perceive His secret plans for the souls of men, and in His goodness they find those gifts of His mercy which are beyond all telling. Yet you must remember Saint Paul's warning as he thanks God for many mighty acts of deliverance, though fearing those judgements and decrees which are as mysterious as the deep. . . . 'But who are you, a man, to answer back to God? Will the pot say to the potter, Why have you made me thus?'[132] Hear, too, when he cries out in wonder at the treasury of God's wisdom: 'O the depth of the riches and wisdom and knowledge of God! How unsearchable are His judgements and how inscrutable His ways!'[133] And when he thinks of all the gifts of God's goodness showered on men, Saint Paul admonishes us not to presume on the riches of that abundant kindness.

CHAPTER FIFTEEN

THE FINDING IN THE TEMPLE

AND so it was only after three days that Jesus was found in the temple, doubtless by Mary and Joseph, His mother and foster-father. And it is in the temple, too, not just anywhere, that the holy man who contemplates the things of the spirit is to be found. For Jerusalem, like so many other cities, has a great space like a courtyard running round the outside of its walls. It has great gates, too, but it also has a temple, which no other city is allowed to have. Sometimes even those who are enemies are allowed to enter its courtyard, though the great gates open only to friends, and only those who are perfect may enter the temple. Now he who can see the reflection of eternity in the things which pass away, who gazes on this world and sees heaven in the things about him, who perceives the image of the Creator in the creatures of God's creation, and for whom human things are like a mirror for the things of God—he, I say, is filled with a great joy, for he has been led into the great courtyard of the heavenly Jerusalem. Even those men who are gifted with great understanding, the philosophers and sages of this world of ours, may come into the courtyard, even though they may be enemies. Saint Paul says that the knowledge of God is clear to their minds, for God Himself has made it clear to them.[134] From the foundation of the world men have caught sight of His invisible nature, His eternal power and His divinity, as they are known through His creatures. But a man who gazes on God's glory face to face in that holy writ which he has understood deeply, has a real reason for happiness and rejoicing, for the gates of the temple have opened and allowed him to enter. Then, when the flame of desire for heaven consumes on the altar of your heart those offerings you make to God (namely, the marrow of closest love[135] and the fatness of your faith and loving devotion) and the sweet incense of your prayer mounts up to God, at last the gaze of your soul rests on the very secrets of heaven, and your heart tastes the sweet savour of God's love. Yes, that is what happens whenever you enter the temple at Jerusalem, and make an offering acceptable and pleasing to God.

But while the holy soul lingers among these delightful pleasures, Christ's mother and foster-father seek for their Son in the greatest distress. At last they find Him, and rebuke Him, as Saint Luke tells us so vividly, and they take Him back to Nazareth with them. And that is just what happens to holy men who have been given souls to look after, or who have been charged to preach the word of God. And I think that for them the Holy Spirit is foster-father, while their mother is none other than Charity herself. Together they shower blessings and kindness on us who have souls in our care, encouraging us to journey on towards God, feeding and nourishing us with the twofold milk of love of God and neighbour. Together they keep and sustain and refresh us as we strive for the things of God, just as Mary and Joseph supported the boy Jesus during the years of His youth at Nazareth. Together they console us when our hearts are full of sorrow. They counsel us when doubts assail us, and they strengthen us when we are tired and weak, healing the contrite heart and binding up its wounds.[136] And if we pass from Nazareth to Jerusalem, from toil to rest, and from the fruit of a good life to the secrets of contemplation, it is because they are always at our side, helping and assisting us.

It is the law of Charity and of the Holy Spirit, that we

must neither neglect the contemplation of God in order to look after our neighbour, nor forsake our neighbour in order to spend all our time in gazing on God. So it is that, if we try to enjoy a little peace and quiet more than we should, or if we linger there too long, fraternal charity complains about us, and is displeased with our staying in Jerusalem when disaster threatens those in our care, while we are resting in the joys of prayer. For often, when we have turned aside from the business and activities that go with our office, and have given our thoughts to prayer and meditation, the Holy Spirit and Charity will strive to arouse us when we linger among these delights a minute longer than is good for those who have been entrusted to our charge. Then suddenly the memory of our weaker sons comes into our minds, and we think of one whose heart is full of woe and who waits for his father to comfort him with love and compassion. Then we remember that another son whom temptation has set about with snares is looking for us, and waiting for us to come out from our prayers to give him some words of comfort and consolation. And we hear in our soul the murmurings of a son against his father, because he is worried by the stings of anger, and has nowhere to kill the poison by a confession that will restore him to health. Then we think of a son whom accidie[137] holds in its grip, and of how he must be running backwards and forwards looking for someone to whom he may speak, and from whom he may beg a little advice and help.

When these promptings have led us from our solitude and prayer, we hear our mother, Charity, rebuking us: 'My Son, why hast Thou treated us so? Think what anguish of mind Thy father and I have endured searching for Thee.' And the Holy Spirit, the love which has its home in the saints, even in those who are not completely perfect, complains to us and is full of sorrow and distress, searching for us. No, it is not wrong to say that He does that, for Saint Paul tells us that the Spirit Himself intercedes for us all with groans beyond all utterance.[138] And so it is that He can speak and sorrow in the saints. Perhaps the soul that loves the peace and rest of prayer will complain of his charge in the face of all these calls, and say deep down in his longing heart: 'Could you not tell that I must needs be in my Father's house?' But then he will remember that Christ died so that we might all learn that a man must not live for himself alone, but also for others. And so he will go with his foster-father, the Holy Spirit, and Charity, his mother, and be subject to them in all obedience. He is full of confidence and trust, for he goes from the temple accompanied by the Holy Spirit and encouraged by Charity, to obey the call of love for those who have been entrusted to him.

Yes, I will be very willing to go even to Egypt, the land of darkness, under their leadership, for if they take me there they will bring me back to the temple again, I know. If they force me to go with them to the land of exile, they will surely lead me back again to my true home. And I shall be happy to serve and obey such masters. Never will I hesitate to put their burden on my shoulders, and take their yoke upon my neck, for I know that their yoke is easy and their burden light.[139] But I know, my dearest son, that Christ keeps you under His wing, away from all such care and responsibilities which lie heavily on superiors, who must see to it that none of their subjects is in any sort of worry or temptation. Yet you must foresee all these things and prepare yourself for the time when you too will have to bear that burden, or else you will shock and scandalize those who are with you in the community. A superior must give first place to the calls of his office, setting them before the delights of contemplation in which he finds such happiness. And you, in your turn, my son, must give first place to the peace and harmony of the community in which you live, preferring that to the great pleasure you have in prayer and contemplation. And lastly, my advice is this: never rely on your own opinion or judgement, but always seek the advice and guidance of wiser members of your community, in discerning the various changes and stages in your spiritual journey, whether it be that you are going down to Nazareth or up to the temple at Jerusalem.

EPILOGUE

AND so, dearest son, here is the little work you asked for, although it is in no way worthy of your expectations, and can hardly satisfy the desire you expressed to me, or the longing which I know you have for our Lord. Yet I think it shows that I have tried my best, and that I want to grant your request. You asked me, not only to explain and interpret this lesson from Saint Luke's gospel, but also to make it bear some seeds of meditation and love, and this I have tried to do. If the thoughts that I have put down here do encourage devotion in those who read this passage from the Gospel, it will be because I have written these lines, such as they are, with the help of Him of Whose childhood I have been speaking, Jesus Christ our Lord, Who with the Father and the Holy Spirit lives and reigns for ever and ever. Amen.

NOTES

1 Luke ii. 42.
2 Job vi. 7.
3 Ps. xli. 4.
4 Matt. xix. 14.
5 Matt. vi. 29–30.
6 Ps. xix. 6.
7 Ps. xviii. 11.
8 Ps. cvii. 10.
9 Luke xv. 11.
10 Ps. xlix. 12.
11 Ps. cvii. 4.
12 Luke xv. 17.
13 Ps. cvii. 7.
14 ibid. 8–9.
15 John vi. 41.
16 Ps. lxxiii. 22.
17 Ecclus. ii. 1.
18 Ps. cvii. 10.
19 Eph. iv. 13.
20 Cant. i. 1.
21 ibid. viii. 1.
22 Cf. Phil. ii. 7.
23 Luke ii. 47.
24 Cant. iii. 4.
25 Luke ii. 48.
26 ibid. ii. 49.
27 ibid. ii. 50–51.
28 ibid. i. 35.
29 ibid. ii. 51.
30 ibid. ii. 52.
31 Our Lord, as man,
   acquired experi-
   mental knowledge
   of the world about
   Him, like other
   men.
32 Ps. cii. 27.
33 John xiv. 6.
34 Cf. Luke xv. 16–17.
35 Ps. cii. 9.
36 John i. 1.
37 Cf. Luke ii. 7.
38 Ps. lxxx. 5.

39 Ps. vii. 13.
40 Ps. xi. 2.
41 Matt. xxii. 37.
42 Luke ii. 43.
43 Gen. xli. 45.
44 Luke ii. 44.
45 Jer. xii. 7–8.
46 Dan. ii. 34–35.
47 Ps. xix. 6.
48 Isa. i. 3.
49 Ps. lxix. 23.
50 Jer. ii. 8.
51 II Cor. iii. 15.
52 Cant. vi. 12.
53 Matt. xii. 47.
54 Isa. x. 21.
55 Hos. iii. 5.
56 Eph. v. 29.
57 Isa. lviii. 7.
58 Gen. iv. 11.
59 Ps. lxxix. 12; cf. Gen.
   iv. 15.
60 Gen. xxv. 23; Rom.
   ix. 12.
61 Ps. lix. 6.
62 Acts xiii. 46.
63 Luke xxiv. 29.
64 Matt. xxiv. 12.
65 I Tim. ii. 5.
66 Gen. xlv. 26.
67 Luke ii. 48.
68 Luke xv. 30
69 Jer. iii. 9.
70 Rom. i. 23.
71 Rom. ix. 5.
72 Ps. cxxxii. 6.
73 Exod. xiv. 21.
74 ibid. xvi; xvii. 6.
75 Jer. vi. 20; x. 13.
76 Luke xxiv. 25–26, 47.
77 Ps. ii. 8.
78 Gen. xxii. 18.

79 Isa. xlix. 6.
80 Gen. xlix. 10.
81 Hag. ii. 8.
82 Mal. i. 11.
83 Rom. xi. 21.
84 Ps. cii. 14.
85 Matt. xxviii. 20.
86 I Cor. iii. 18.
87 Matt. xviii. 3.
88 I Peter ii. 11.
89 Wisd. viii. 7.
90 Isa. xi. 2.
91 Ps. xlv. 2.
92 Cant. II, 9.
93 ibid. IV, 7.
94 ibid. IV, 11.
95 ibid. II, 12.
96 ibid. III, 1.
97 I Kings xix. 11–13.
98 Cant. III, 6.
99 Matt. vi. 6.
100 Ps. xlv. 2.
101 Cant. II, 13.
102 Ps. xlii. 4.
103 Cant. III, 4.
104 Eccles. ii. 1.
105 Gen. xl. 14.
106 Ps. xxxi. 19.
107 Ps. xxiv. 8.
108 Job ix. 13; xii. 15.
109 Ps. xxxv. 2.
110 Jer. i. 8.
111 Ps. lxxiii. 3.
112 Jer. xii. 1.
113 Ps. xciv. 10.
114 Rev. iii. 7.
115 Deut. xxxiii. 2.
116 Ps. xlv. 6.
117 Ps. xxvii. 8.
118 Cant. VIII, 1.
119 ibid. I, 3.
120 Ps. xlv. 2.

[121] Luke vii. 36–50.
[122] Gen. iii. 15.
[123] John xii. 13.
[124] II Cor. ii. 16.
[125] Jer. xiii. 23.
[126] Luke vii. 39.
[127] Matt. ix. 20.
[128] Luke vii. 47.
[129] Ps. lxxi. 16.
[130] Ps. li. 6.

[131] Ps. lxiii. 3.
[132] Rom. ix. 20.
[133] Rom. xi. 33.
[134] Rom. i. 19–20.
[135] Ps. lxiii. 5.
[136] Ps. cxlvii. 3.
[137] Accidie means spiritual sloth, or weariness in well-doing. Cassian devotes the tenth book of his *Institutes* to this temptation and the methods for overcoming it. Saint Thomas treats of it in the *Summa theologica* II. ii. 35.
[138] Rom. viii. 26
[139] Matt. xi. 30.